ACE THE INTERVIEW

Strategies to Stand Out and
Secure Your Dream Job

Swanky View

Swanky View

CONTENTS

I. INTRODUCTION

Job interviews are a crucial step in the hiring process, as they provide an opportunity for both the employer and the candidate to assess each other's suitability for the role. They not only gauge your technical skills and qualifications but also give the employer a glimpse into your personality, work ethic, and cultural fit within the organization.

During a job interview, the employer can evaluate your communication skills, professionalism, and ability to think on your feet. The interviewer can ask you specific questions about your background, experience, and qualifications to better understand how you could fit into the company's culture and contribute to its success. The interview can also provide a chance for the employer to clarify any questions or concerns they may have about your application, which could ultimately affect the final hiring decision.

For the candidate, job interviews are an opportunity to showcase their skills and experience, demonstrate their interest and enthusiasm for the role, and ask questions about the position and the company. Interviews are also an excellent opportunity for candidates to learn more about the company culture, values, and work environment, allowing them to determine if the job is the right fit for their career goals and aspirations.

In addition, job interviews can be a valuable learning experience, even if you are not offered the position. The feedback and insights gained from the interview can help you identify areas for improvement and prepare better for future job interviews.

A. Importance Of Job Interviews

Job interviews play a critical role in the hiring process, and their importance cannot be overstated. A job interview is a chance for the employer to get to know the candidate better, assess their qualifications and experience, and evaluate their suitability for the position. At the same time, it is also an opportunity for the candidate to demonstrate their skills, showcase their experience and personality, and express their enthusiasm for the role.

The importance of job interviews lies in the fact that they allow employers to evaluate the candidate beyond their resume and cover letter. A job interview provides the employer with a chance to see how the candidate communicates, behaves, and interacts with others. By asking questions, the interviewer can better understand the candidate's thought process, problem-solving skills, and decision-making abilities.

Job interviews also provide an opportunity for the candidate to learn more about the company, its culture, and the role. This can help them determine if the job is the right fit for them and make an informed decision about accepting the position.

Another critical aspect of job interviews is that they help employers and candidates establish a rapport and build trust. By meeting face-to-face, the employer and the candidate can establish a personal connection and develop a better understanding of each other's needs and expectations. This can lead to a more positive hiring experience and set the foundation for a successful working relationship.

B. Purpose Of The Book

The purpose of "Ace the Interview: Strategies to Stand Out and Secure Your Dream Job" is to provide comprehensive guidance for acing job interviews. This book is designed to help job seekers at all stages of their careers, whether they are fresh graduates or experienced professionals, to prepare for job interviews with confidence and poise.

The book is structured to cover all aspects of the job interview process, from research and preparation to follow-ups. It provides practical tips and strategies for answering common interview questions, showcasing your unique selling proposition, and navigating difficult interview situations. The book also includes guidance on interview etiquette, dressing for success, and communicating your strengths and achievements.

The purpose of the book is to help job seekers stand out from other candidates and secure their dream job. By following the strategies and techniques outlined in this book, readers will be better equipped to handle the challenges and uncertainties of the job search process and increase their chances of success.

The book also aims to foster a positive mindset towards job interviews, viewing them as opportunities to showcase talents and connect with potential employers. By adopting this outlook, readers will be better prepared to handle the stress and anxiety that can come with job interviews and approach them with confidence and resilience.

II. PREPARING FOR THE INTERVIEW

P reparing for an interview is crucial in ensuring that you present yourself in the best light possible to your potential employer. Here are some tips to help you prepare:

A. Researching The Company And Role

One of the essential steps in preparing for a job interview is researching the company and the role you are applying for. By doing your homework, you will gain valuable insights into the company's culture, values, and goals, as well as the role's responsibilities and requirements. This will allow you to tailor your responses during the interview and demonstrate your understanding of the company and the role.

To start, visit the company's website and social media pages, read their mission statement, and learn about their products or services. Look for any recent news or press releases that may be relevant to the role you are applying for. You can also check out industry publications or news sites to gain a broader perspective on the company's position in the market.

Next, review the job description carefully and make a list of the required skills and qualifications. Identify any areas where you may need to improve your skills or knowledge to meet the job requirements. You can also reach out to current or former employees of the company or industry experts to gain more insights into the role and the company's culture.

During the interview, demonstrate your research by asking insightful questions about the company and the role. Show that you have a genuine interest in the company and are committed to its mission and values. By doing so, you will demonstrate your preparedness and enthusiasm for the role, which can set you apart from other candidates.

1. Understanding The Company's Mission And Values

Understanding the company's mission and values is a crucial aspect of researching the company before a job interview. The company's mission statement outlines its core purpose and goals, while its values define the company's culture and priorities. By familiarizing yourself with these elements, you can gain insights into what the company stands for, its priorities, and its approach to business.

To understand the company's mission and values, start by visiting the company's website and reading its mission statement. This statement usually highlights the company's overall purpose, such as its vision or commitment to serving its customers. You can also look for information on the company's core values, which may be listed on the website or in company publications.

Understanding the company's mission and values is essential

because it can help you tailor your responses during the interview to align with the company's goals and values. For example, if the company values innovation and creativity, you can emphasize your experience in these areas and provide examples of how you have used them to achieve success in previous roles. If the company values teamwork and collaboration, you can highlight your experience working in a team environment and how you have contributed to the success of the team.

During the interview, you can also ask questions that demonstrate your understanding of the company's mission and values. For example, you can ask about the company's approach to corporate social responsibility or how it supports its employees' professional development. This shows that you are committed to the company's mission and values and are interested in being part of its culture and community.

2. Identifying Key Responsibilities Of The Role

Identifying the key responsibilities of the role is an essential step in researching the company before a job interview. By understanding the role's responsibilities, you can demonstrate your relevant skills and experience during the interview and show how you can contribute to the company's success.

To identify the key responsibilities of the role, start by reviewing the job description carefully. The job description usually outlines the role's primary responsibilities and requirements, such as managing a team, overseeing projects, or developing new products. Pay attention to any specific skills or qualifications required for the role, such as experience in a particular industry or proficiency in a specific software program.

Next, research the company's industry and competitors to gain a broader perspective on the role's responsibilities. Look for trends and challenges in the industry that may affect the role and the company's success. Identify areas where you can leverage your skills and experience to help the company overcome these challenges.

During the interview, be prepared to discuss your experience and skills relevant to the role's responsibilities. Use specific examples from your previous roles to demonstrate how you have handled similar responsibilities and achieved success. Be prepared to answer questions about how you would approach specific aspects of the role, such as managing a team or handling a challenging project.

B. Analyzing Job Requirements And Matching Them With Your Skills

Analyzing the job requirements and matching them with your skills is a critical step in preparing for a job interview. By doing so, you can identify any gaps in your skills or experience and develop a plan to address them before the interview. This will help you demonstrate your relevant skills and experience during the interview and show how you can contribute to the company's success.

To analyze the job requirements, start by carefully reviewing the job description and identifying the required skills, experience, and qualifications. Look for specific keywords and phrases that indicate what the company is looking for in a candidate. Pay attention to any certifications or degrees required for the role, as well as any specific software programs or technologies you need to be proficient in.

Next, evaluate your own skills and experience and identify areas where you match the job requirements. Use specific examples from your previous roles to demonstrate your relevant skills and achievements. Be honest about any gaps in your skills or experience, and develop a plan to address them before the interview. This could include taking a course, getting certified, or gaining relevant experience through volunteering or freelance work.

During the interview, be prepared to discuss your relevant skills and experience and demonstrate how you can apply them to the role. Use specific examples to show how you have handled similar responsibilities in the past and achieved success. Be honest about any gaps in your skills or experience, but demonstrate a willingness to learn and grow in the role.

C. Preparing Your Elevator Pitch

Preparing your elevator pitch is an essential step in preparing for a job interview. An elevator pitch is a concise and compelling summary of who you are, what you do, and what you can bring to the company. It is called an elevator pitch because it should be short enough to deliver in the time it takes to ride an elevator.

To prepare your elevator pitch, start by identifying your unique selling proposition or what sets you apart from other candidates. This could be your experience, skills, achievements, or a combination of factors. Develop a brief statement that summarizes your unique selling proposition and communicates your value to the company.

Next, practice delivering your elevator pitch in a clear and confident manner. Make sure it is concise and easy to understand, using simple language and avoiding jargon or technical terms. Practice in front of a mirror or with a friend or family member to get feedback on your delivery and refine your pitch.

During the interview, be prepared to deliver your elevator pitch when the interviewer asks you to tell them about yourself. This is a common opening question, and a well-crafted elevator pitch can make a positive first impression and set the tone for the rest of the interview.

D. Gathering Relevant Documents

Gathering relevant documents is an essential step in preparing for a job interview. Having all the necessary documents ready and organized beforehand will save you time and reduce stress on the day of the interview. It will also demonstrate your preparedness and professionalism to the interviewer.

To gather relevant documents, start by reviewing the job description and identifying any documents you may need to bring to the interview. This could include a copy of your resume, cover letter, references, certifications, diplomas, or any other relevant documents.

Make sure your resume is up to date and tailored to the job you are applying for. Review your cover letter and make any necessary changes to customize it to the company and the role.

Next, gather all the necessary documents and organize them in a folder or portfolio. Label each document clearly, so you can quickly find what you need during the interview. Make sure you have extra copies of your resume and cover letter in case the interviewer requests them.

It is also a good idea to bring a notepad and pen to take notes during the interview. This will show the interviewer that you are engaged and interested in the role.

During the interview, refer to your documents as needed and offer them to the interviewer if requested. Being organized and prepared will demonstrate your professionalism and attention to detail.

1. Resume And Cover Letter

The resume and cover letter are two of the most important documents you need to bring to a job interview. They are often the first documents the interviewer will see, and they provide a snapshot of your skills, experience, and qualifications.

Your resume should be up to date and tailored to the job you are applying for. Highlight your relevant skills and experience, and use specific examples to demonstrate your achievements. Make sure your resume is easy to read, with clear headings and bullet points to break up the text.

Your cover letter should also be tailored to the company and the role. It should provide a brief overview of your relevant experience and qualifications, and explain why you are a good fit for the role. Use specific examples to demonstrate your interest in the company and its mission, and explain how your skills and experience align with the job requirements.

Before the interview, review your resume and cover letter carefully and make any necessary changes. Ensure that there are no typos or errors, and that the formatting is consistent throughout. Bring extra copies of your resume and cover letter in case the interviewer requests them.

During the interview, refer to your resume and cover letter

as needed and be prepared to answer questions about your skills and experience. Use specific examples to demonstrate your achievements and show how your skills align with the job requirements.

2. References And Recommendation Letters

References and recommendation letters are additional documents that you may need to bring to a job interview. They provide additional information about your skills, experience, and character and can help demonstrate your suitability for the role.

References are people who can speak to your skills, experience, and character. They may be former employers, colleagues, or mentors who have worked with you in the past. Before the interview, ask your references for their permission to be contacted by the interviewer and provide them with a copy of the job description so that they can speak to your suitability for the role.

Recommendation letters are letters written by former employers, colleagues, or mentors that endorse your skills and experience. They provide additional details about your performance, work ethic, and character and can help demonstrate your suitability for the role. If you have recommendation letters, bring them to the interview and offer them to the interviewer if requested.

When selecting references and recommendation letters to bring to the interview, choose people who can speak to your relevant skills and experience. Ensure that they are up to date and relevant to the job you are applying for. Before the interview, review them carefully and be prepared to discuss their contents with the interviewer.

During the interview, be prepared to offer your references and recommendation letters if requested. Provide the interviewer with their contact information and explain how they can speak to your suitability for the role. Use their feedback to demonstrate your relevant skills and experience and show how they align with the job requirements.

3. Certificates And Licenses

Certificates and licenses are additional documents that you may need to bring to a job interview, depending on the job requirements. They demonstrate that you have completed a training program or have met certain professional standards and can help demonstrate your expertise in a particular area.

Certificates are documents that show that you have completed a training program or course. They may be relevant to the job you are applying for, such as a certificate in project management or a certification in a particular software program. Before the interview, review your certificates and ensure that they are up to date and relevant to the job.

Licenses are documents that show that you have met certain professional standards and are authorized to practice in a particular field. They may be required for certain jobs, such as a driver's license for a delivery driver or a professional license for a nurse. Before the interview, ensure that your licenses are up to date and relevant to the job.

When bringing certificates and licenses to the interview, make sure to organize them and label them clearly. Bring extra copies in case the interviewer requests them.

During the interview, be prepared to discuss your certificates and licenses and how they relate to the job requirements. Use specific examples to demonstrate how you have used your training or professional standards to achieve success in previous roles. Provide the interviewer with copies of your certificates and licenses if requested.

III. DRESSING
FOR SUCCESS

Dressing for success is an important aspect of preparing for a job interview. Your appearance can create a positive or negative impression on the interviewer, and can influence their perception of your professionalism, attention to detail, and overall suitability for the job.

When deciding what to wear to a job interview, it is important to consider the company culture and dress code. Research the company and try to get a sense of its culture and how employees typically dress. If in doubt, it is usually better to err on the side of dressing more formally than too casually.

A good rule of thumb is to dress in business professional attire, which includes a suit or dress pants and a jacket for men and a suit or a professional dress for women. Choose clothing that is clean, pressed, and fits well. Avoid clothing that is too tight, too revealing, or too casual.

In addition to your clothing, pay attention to your grooming and accessories. Make sure your hair is neat and tidy, your nails are clean and trimmed, and your shoes are polished and in good condition. Keep jewelry and accessories to a minimum, and avoid anything too flashy or distracting.

Finally, make sure you are comfortable in what you are wearing. You want to be able to move freely and feel confident during the interview. If you are not used to wearing formal attire, try it on beforehand to ensure that it fits well and feels comfortable.

A. Dress Code Expectations

Dress code expectations can vary depending on the company culture and the type of job you are applying for. It is important to research the company and get a sense of its dress code expectations before the interview.

In a formal or corporate environment, the dress code is usually business professional, which includes a suit or dress pants and a jacket for men, and a suit or a professional dress for women. This dress code is typically associated with traditional, conservative industries such as law, finance, or consulting.

In a business casual environment, the dress code is more relaxed, but still professional. Men may wear a dress shirt and slacks or khakis, while women may wear a blouse and dress pants or a skirt. This dress code is often associated with industries such as marketing, advertising, or technology.

In a casual environment, the dress code may be very relaxed, allowing for jeans and t-shirts. However, it is still important to dress neatly and avoid clothing that is too revealing or distracting.

When deciding what to wear to a job interview, it is always better to err on the side of dressing more formally than too casually. Even if the company has a more casual dress code, it is still important to present a professional appearance to the interviewer.

B. Choosing The Right Attire

Choosing the right attire for a job interview is important because it can influence the interviewer's perception of your professionalism and suitability for the job. Here are some tips for choosing the right attire:

1. Research the company culture and dress code expectations. As mentioned earlier, it is important to research the company and get a sense of its dress code expectations before the interview. This will help you choose the right attire and avoid any missteps.

2. Dress conservatively. Even if the company has a more casual dress code, it is still important to present a professional appearance to the interviewer. This means avoiding clothing that is too revealing or distracting, and opting for more conservative styles.

3. Choose clothing that fits well. Ill-fitting clothing can be distracting and make you feel uncomfortable during the interview. Make sure your clothing fits well and is tailored to your body type.

4. Avoid flashy or distracting accessories. Keep jewelry and accessories to a minimum, and avoid anything too flashy or distracting. Opt for more conservative styles that complement your attire.

5. Dress for the job you want. Choose attire that is appropriate for the job you are applying for, and that reflects your professionalism and suitability for the role. Dressing for the job you want can help you project confidence and competence during the interview.

C. Grooming And Personal Hygiene

Grooming and personal hygiene are important aspects of preparing for a job interview. Your appearance and personal hygiene can make a significant impact on the interviewer's perception of your professionalism, attention to detail, and overall suitability for the job.

Here are some tips for grooming and personal hygiene:

1. Shower or bathe before the interview. This will help you feel clean and refreshed and can help you project confidence and professionalism during the interview.

2. Ensure your hair is neat and tidy. Make sure your hair is clean, styled appropriately, and neatly trimmed. Avoid overly trendy hairstyles or colors that could be distracting.

3. Keep facial hair neat and trimmed. If you have facial hair, make sure it is neatly trimmed and well-groomed. Avoid excessive or unkempt facial hair, which can be distracting or unprofessional.

4. Wear clean, pressed clothing. Make sure your clothing is clean, pressed, and free of wrinkles or stains. This will demonstrate your attention to detail and professionalism to the interviewer.

5. Pay attention to your nails. Make sure your nails are clean and neatly trimmed. Avoid overly long nails or bright nail polish colors that could be distracting.

6. Use deodorant and avoid excessive perfume or cologne. Use deodorant to help control body odor, but avoid using excessive amounts of perfume or cologne, which can be overwhelming and distracting.

7. Brush your teeth and use mouthwash. Good oral hygiene is essential for a job interview. Brush your teeth and use mouthwash to ensure your breath is fresh and clean.

IV. MASTERING INTERVIEW ETIQUETTE

During an interview, it is important to be polite, professional, and respectful. This includes greeting your interviewer with a firm handshake, maintaining eye contact, and using proper language and tone. Here are some tips on to help you master Interview Etiquette:

A. Arriving On Time

Arriving on time for a job interview is crucial to making a good first impression. Being punctual shows the interviewer that you value their time and are committed to the position you are applying for. Additionally, arriving early gives you time to compose yourself, review your notes, and mentally prepare for the interview.

To ensure you arrive on time, it's important to plan ahead. Research the location of the interview and consider the traffic or public transportation schedules that may affect your arrival time. If possible, do a test run to the location before the day of the interview to get a sense of the route and timing.

If you're not familiar with the location, make sure to give yourself extra time to navigate any unexpected challenges that may arise, such as getting lost or finding parking. It's better to arrive too early than to be late, as being late can give the impression that you are not organized or reliable.

If an unforeseen circumstance arises and you know you will be late, be sure to contact the interviewer as soon as possible to let them know. Apologize for the delay and explain the situation. It's better to be honest and transparent than to leave the interviewer waiting and wondering where you are.

B. Making A Great First Impression

1. Body language

Body language is an important aspect of communication, especially during a job interview. The way you carry yourself and present yourself through nonverbal cues can convey confidence, enthusiasm, and professionalism. Conversely, negative body language can undermine your credibility and make the interviewer doubt your suitability for the position.

To project positive body language during an interview, start by making eye contact. This shows that you are engaged and interested in the conversation. Avoid looking down or shifting your gaze around the room, as this can suggest nervousness or disinterest.

Sitting up straight and leaning slightly forward can also convey confidence and engagement. Slouching or leaning too far back can give the impression that you are bored or uninterested.

Smiling can also be a powerful way to project positivity and enthusiasm. However, be mindful not to overdo it, as a constant smile can come across as insincere or inappropriate.

Additionally, avoid fidgeting or touching your face or hair excessively, as this can be distracting and undermine your credibility. Use hand gestures sparingly and purposefully, and keep them at a comfortable distance from your body.

Finally, mirroring the interviewer's body language can be a subtle but effective way to establish rapport and build a connection. This involves subtly mimicking their posture and gestures in a natural and unobtrusive way.

2. Introductions and handshakes

Making a good first impression is critical in a job interview, and your introduction and handshake are important elements of that impression. An effective introduction can help establish rapport with the interviewer and set the tone for a positive conversation, while a handshake can convey confidence, professionalism, and respect.

When you meet the interviewer, approach with a confident and positive attitude. Make eye contact and smile to establish a friendly and engaging demeanor. If there is a desk or table between you, extend your hand to shake theirs while introducing yourself.

For example, "Hi, my name is John. It's great to meet you."

When shaking hands, grip firmly but not too tightly, and shake for two or three pumps. This shows that you are confident and professional without being overbearing or aggressive. Avoid limp or weak handshakes, as these can be interpreted as a lack of confidence or enthusiasm.

It's also important to be attentive to cultural differences and preferences. In some cultures, a firm handshake may be seen as inappropriate or overly aggressive, while in others, a light touch or bow may be more appropriate. If you are unsure, it's always best to err on the side of caution and follow the interviewer's lead.

If the interviewer doesn't offer their hand for a handshake, don't take it personally or read too much into it. They may simply have a preference for other forms of greeting, or they may not be comfortable with physical contact.

C. Active Listening And Effective Communication

Active listening and effective communication are essential skills in a job interview, as they demonstrate your ability to understand and engage with the interviewer's questions and concerns. By listening actively and communicating effectively, you can establish rapport with the interviewer, demonstrate your suitability for the position, and increase your chances of landing the job.

Active listening involves more than just hearing the interviewer's questions. It involves paying attention to their tone, body language, and nonverbal cues, as well as the words they use. Focus on the interviewer's message and avoid interrupting or thinking about your own responses before they have finished speaking. Take notes if necessary to help you remember important points.

Effective communication involves more than just giving a clear answer. It involves tailoring your response to the interviewer's question, communicating your thoughts and ideas clearly and concisely, and using appropriate language and tone. Avoid jargon or overly technical language, as this can be off-putting to the interviewer. Instead, use plain language and examples to illustrate your points.

When answering questions, be sure to provide relevant and specific examples from your work experience. This helps to demonstrate your skills and expertise in a tangible way. Use the STAR method (Situation, Task, Action, Result) to structure your responses and make them easy to follow.

Finally, don't be afraid to ask questions or seek clarification if you don't understand something. This demonstrates your interest in the position and your willingness to engage with the interviewer. It can also help to clarify any misunderstandings and ensure that you are on the same page.

D. Asking Thoughtful Questions

Asking thoughtful questions during a job interview is an important way to demonstrate your interest in the position, engage with the interviewer, and gain valuable insights into the company and its culture. By asking insightful questions, you can show your enthusiasm for the role, demonstrate your knowledge of the industry, and help to establish a rapport with the interviewer.

When preparing questions to ask, consider the job requirements and the company's mission and values. Tailor your questions to these areas to show that you have done your research and are genuinely interested in the position.

Here are a few examples of thoughtful questions to ask during a job interview:

1. What are the biggest challenges facing this department or organization right now, and how do you see the successful candidate helping to address them?
2. How do you see this role evolving over time, and what opportunities are there for professional growth and development within the company?
3. Can you describe the company culture and how it supports the mission and values of the organization?
4. What is the management style of the supervisor for this role, and what do they value in their team members?
5. How does the company foster a sense of community and teamwork among employees?

When asking questions, be sure to listen carefully to the interviewer's responses and engage in a genuine conversation. Don't ask questions simply for the sake of asking them or to show off your knowledge. Instead, use your questions to demonstrate your enthusiasm for the role and to gain valuable insights into the company and its culture.

V. ANSWERING COMMON INTERVIEW QUESTIONS

A. Behavioral Questions

Behavioral questions are a common type of interview question that asks you to describe how you have responded to specific situations in the past. These questions are designed to assess your problem-solving skills, your ability to work in a team, and your general approach to work.

When answering behavioral questions, it's important to use the STAR method (Situation, Task, Action, Result) to structure your responses. This helps you to provide a clear and concise answer and ensures that you cover all the necessary elements of the question.

Here's an example of how to use the STAR method to answer a behavioral question:

Question: Can you describe a time when you had to work with a difficult colleague, and how you handled the situation?

Situation: "I was working on a team project with a colleague who had a tendency to be confrontational and dismissive of other people's ideas."

Task: "My task was to find a way to work with this colleague and keep the project on track."

Action: "I scheduled a meeting with the colleague to discuss our work styles and how we could work together more effectively. During the meeting, I listened actively to their concerns and acknowledged their ideas. I also shared my own perspective and suggested ways we could collaborate more effectively."

Result: "After the meeting, we were able to find common ground and work together more effectively. The project was completed on time and to a high standard."

When answering behavioral questions, it's important to be specific and provide relevant details. Use concrete examples from your work experience to illustrate your points and demonstrate your skills and expertise. Avoid using vague or generic statements, as these can be less compelling and make it harder for the interviewer to assess your suitability for the role.

B. Situational Questions

Situational questions are a type of interview question that presents you with a hypothetical scenario and asks how you would respond. These questions are designed to assess your problem-solving skills, your ability to think on your feet, and your general approach to work.

When answering situational questions, it's important to follow a structured approach.

Here's an example of how to approach a situational question using the SOAR method (Situation, Obstacle, Action, Result):

Question: "Imagine that you are leading a project team and one of your team members is consistently missing deadlines. What would you do?"

Situation: "One of my project team members is consistently missing deadlines."
Obstacle: "This is impacting the project timeline and causing delays."

Action: "I would schedule a meeting with the team member to discuss the situation and understand why they are missing deadlines. During the meeting, I would listen actively to their concerns and work with them to identify any obstacles that are preventing them from meeting their deadlines. I would also work with them to develop a plan to get back on track and meet the project goals."

Result: "By taking a proactive approach and addressing the issue head-on, we were able to get the project back on track and meet our goals. The team member was able to overcome the obstacles and contribute to the success of the project."

When answering situational questions, it's important to be specific and provide relevant details. Use concrete examples from your work experience to illustrate your points and demonstrate your skills and expertise. Avoid using vague or generic statements, as these can be less compelling and make it harder for the interviewer to assess your suitability for the role.

C. Technical Questions

Technical questions are a type of interview question that assesses your knowledge and expertise in a specific field or skillset. These questions are designed to assess your technical skills, problem-solving abilities, and your approach to solving complex issues.

When answering technical questions, it's important to be honest and transparent about your level of expertise. If you don't know the answer to a question, it's better to admit it than to try to bluff your way through.

Here are a few tips for answering technical questions during a job interview:

1. Prepare beforehand: Review the job requirements and identify the technical skills and knowledge that are required for the position. Study up on these areas beforehand and be prepared to answer technical questions related to them.

2. Listen carefully to the question: Make sure you fully understand the technical question being asked before answering. Take a moment to clarify the question with the interviewer if needed.

3. Use relevant examples: Use concrete examples from your work experience to illustrate your technical skills and knowledge. This can help to demonstrate your expertise in a tangible way.

4. Be honest about your limitations: If you don't know

the answer to a technical question, be honest and transparent about it. You can offer to research the topic further and follow up with the interviewer after the interview.

5. Show your problem-solving skills: Even if you don't know the answer to a technical question, you can demonstrate your problem-solving skills by talking through your thought process and how you would approach solving the problem.

D. Problem-Solving Questions

Problem-solving questions are a type of interview question that presents you with a hypothetical scenario and asks how you would approach solving the problem. These questions are designed to assess your problem-solving skills, your ability to think critically, and your approach to tackling complex issues.

When answering problem-solving questions, it's important to follow a structured approach.

Here's an example of how to approach a problem-solving question using the PAPA method (Problem, Action, Pros, and Cons, and Alternative solutions):

Question: "You are given a complex problem that has no obvious solution. How would you approach solving it?"

Problem: "The first step in problem-solving is to clearly define the problem. Take some time to analyze the problem and identify what needs to be solved."

Action: "After identifying the problem, brainstorm potential solutions. Use creative thinking and consider all possible options."

Pros and Cons: "Evaluate each potential solution by weighing the pros and cons. Identify the potential benefits and drawbacks of each solution."

Alternative Solutions: "Based on the pros and cons, select the most viable solution and outline the steps you would take to implement it. However, also present alternative solutions that can be considered."

When answering problem-solving questions, it's important to be specific and provide relevant details. Use concrete examples from your work experience to illustrate your points and demonstrate your skills and expertise.

Avoid using vague or generic statements, as these can be less compelling and make it harder for the interviewer to assess your suitability for the role.

E. Personal Questions

Personal questions are a type of interview question that seeks to assess your personality, work style, and personal values. These questions are designed to assess how you might fit into the company culture and work with the team.

When answering personal questions, it's important to be honest and authentic.

Here are some tips for answering personal questions during a job interview:

1. Be yourself: Personal questions are designed to assess your personality, so it's important to be authentic and let your personality shine through. Be honest about your values, interests, and work style.

2. Be positive: When answering personal questions, try to focus on the positive aspects of your personality and work style. Highlight your strengths and how they can contribute to the company's success.

3. Use examples: Use concrete examples from your work experience to illustrate your personality traits and work style. This can help to demonstrate your suitability for the role in a tangible way.

4. Stay professional: While personal questions are designed to assess your personality, it's important to remain professional and avoid oversharing. Keep your answers relevant to the job requirements and the company culture.

5. Be aware of biases: Personal questions can sometimes be used to assess characteristics that may not be relevant to the job requirements or the company culture. Be aware of any biases that may be present in the questions and answer them truthfully and authentically.

VI. SHOWCASING YOUR UNIQUE SELLING PROPOSITION

A. Identifying Your Differentiators

Identifying your differentiators is an important step in preparing for a job interview. Differentiators are the unique qualities, skills, and experiences that set you apart from other candidates and make you a strong fit for the position.

When identifying your differentiators, start by reviewing the job requirements and the company's mission and

values. Think about your skills, experiences, and personal qualities that align with these areas.

Here are a few tips for identifying your differentiators:

1. Consider your strengths: Think about the skills and experiences that make you stand out. What do you excel at? What sets you apart from other candidates? Use

these strengths to showcase why you are the best fit for the job.

2. Look for unique experiences: Consider any unique experiences you have that are relevant to the job. For example, if the job requires experience working with a specific software program, highlight your experience with that program and how it can be valuable to the company.

3. Use stories: Use real-life examples and stories to demonstrate how your differentiators have helped you succeed in previous roles. This can help to illustrate your skills and experiences in a tangible way.

4. Be authentic: While it's important to identify your differentiators, it's also important to be authentic and honest. Don't exaggerate your skills or experiences, and focus on what truly sets you apart.

5. Use keywords: Use keywords from the job description and the company's mission and values when describing your differentiators. This can help to demonstrate how your skills and experiences align with the position and the company culture.

B. Communicating Your Strengths

Communicating your strengths is an essential part of succeeding in a job interview. Your strengths are the qualities and skills that make you a valuable asset to the company, and highlighting them can help to demonstrate why you are the best fit for the position.

When communicating your strengths, it's important to focus on the specific skills and experiences that are relevant to the job requirements.

Here are a few tips for effectively communicating your strengths during a job interview:

1. Be specific: When discussing your strengths, be specific and provide concrete examples. Use specific achievements and accomplishments to demonstrate how your strengths can contribute to the company's success.

2. Use keywords: Use keywords from the job description and the company's mission and values when discussing your strengths. This can help to demonstrate how your skills and experiences align with the position and the company culture.

3. Be confident: When discussing your strengths, be confident and assertive. Use a confident tone of voice and body language to demonstrate your conviction in your skills and experiences.

4. Avoid arrogance: While it's important to be confident, it's also important to avoid coming across as arrogant or overconfident. Use a humble tone and avoid exaggerating your accomplishments.

5. Use the STAR method: Use the STAR method (Situation, Task, Action, Result) to structure your responses when discussing your strengths. This can help to provide a clear and concise answer and ensure that you cover all the necessary elements of the question.

C. Providing Concrete Examples Of Your Achievements

Providing concrete examples of your achievements is an effective way to demonstrate your skills and experiences during a job interview. Concrete examples can help to illustrate how you have applied your skills and experiences in real-life situations, and provide evidence of your capabilities.

When providing concrete examples of your achievements, it's important to focus on the specific achievements that are relevant to the job requirements.

Here are a few tips for effectively providing concrete examples of your achievements during a job interview:

1. Be specific: When discussing your achievements, be specific and provide concrete examples. Use specific achievements and accomplishments to demonstrate how your skills and experiences can contribute to the company's success.

2. Use metrics: Use metrics to quantify your achievements whenever possible. For example, if you improved sales performance, state the percentage increase in sales.

3. Provide context: Provide context for your achievements to help the interviewer understand the significance of your accomplishments. Explain the challenges you faced, the actions you took, and the results you achieved.

4. Use the STAR method: Use the STAR method (Situation, Task, Action, Result) to structure your responses when providing examples of your achievements. This can help to provide a clear and concise answer and ensure that you cover all the necessary elements of the question.

5. Relate to the job requirements: Whenever possible, relate your achievements to the job requirements. Explain how your achievements demonstrate your ability to succeed in the position.

VII. NAVIGATING DIFFICULT INTERVIEW SITUATIONS

Difficult interview situations can arise unexpectedly, such as being asked a question you don't know the answer to or being faced with an uncomfortable topic. It's important to stay calm, composed, and honest in these situations, and to turn them into opportunities to show your problem-solving and critical thinking skills. Here are some tips to help you overcome these interview situations:

A. Handling Unexpected Questions

Handling unexpected questions during a job interview can be challenging, but it's important to stay calm and composed. Unexpected questions can range from personal questions to technical questions outside of your expertise, and they are often designed to assess your ability to think on your feet and handle pressure.

When faced with an unexpected question, here are a few tips to help you handle it with confidence:

1. Take a breath: Before answering the question, take a moment to breathe and compose yourself. This can help you to gather your thoughts and respond in a calm and collected manner.

2. Clarify the question: If the question is unclear or you need more information, don't hesitate to ask for clarification. This can help you to better understand the question and respond more effectively.

3. Be honest: If you don't know the answer to an unexpected question, be honest and transparent. Don't try to bluff your way through or make up an answer. Instead, admit that you don't know and offer to follow up with more information after the interview.

4. Stay focused: Try to stay focused on the interview and the job requirements, even when faced with unexpected questions. Keep in mind the key skills and experiences that are required for the position and use them to guide your responses.

5. Be confident: Even when faced with unexpected questions, try to remain confident and assertive. Use a confident tone of voice and body language to demonstrate your conviction in your skills and experiences.

B. Addressing Employment Gaps And Career Changes

Addressing employment gaps and career changes during a job interview can be challenging, but it's important to be honest and provide a clear explanation. Employers may view employment gaps and career changes as red flags, but by addressing them proactively, you can demonstrate your professionalism and commitment to your career.

When addressing employment gaps, here are a few tips to help you navigate the conversation:

1. Be honest: Be honest and transparent about the reasons for your employment gap. Explain the circumstances that led to the gap and what you did during that time.

2. Focus on the positives: While employment gaps can be viewed negatively, try to focus on the positive aspects of the experience. For example, you may have used the time to gain new skills or take courses to improve your knowledge.

3. Highlight volunteer work or freelance projects: If you were not employed during the gap, highlight any volunteer work or freelance projects you worked on during that time. This can demonstrate your commitment to staying active and engaged in your career.

4. Explain how you stayed current: If you were not working during the gap, explain how you stayed current in your field. For example, you may have attended conferences or industry events, or stayed up-to-date on the latest trends and developments.

When addressing career changes, here are a few tips to help you navigate the conversation:

1. Explain your motivation: Explain why you decided to make the career change and what motivated you to pursue the new path.

2. Highlight transferable skills: Highlight the transferable skills and experiences that you can bring to the new role. This can demonstrate how your previous experience can be valuable in the new position.

3. Explain how you prepared for the change: Explain how you prepared for the career change, such as taking courses, attending networking events, or working on side projects.

4. Show enthusiasm: Show enthusiasm for the new career path and demonstrate your commitment to making the transition successfully.

C. Discussing Salary Expectations

Discussing salary expectations during a job interview can be uncomfortable, but it's important to be prepared and have a clear understanding of your worth in the market. Salary negotiations are a crucial part of the hiring process and can impact your long-term earning potential, so it's important to approach the conversation with confidence and professionalism.

Here are some tips for discussing salary expectations during a job interview:

1. Research salary ranges: Before the interview, research salary ranges for the position and location. This can help you to determine a reasonable salary range based on your skills, experience, and qualifications.

2. Consider your priorities: Consider your priorities beyond salary, such as benefits, flexible work arrangements, and opportunities for growth and development. This can help you to negotiate a package that is more aligned with your overall career goals.

3. Be confident: When discussing salary expectations, be confident and assertive. Use a confident tone of voice and body language to demonstrate your conviction in your value.

4. Be open to negotiation: Be prepared to negotiate and have a range in mind that you are comfortable with. This can show the employer that you are flexible and open to finding a mutually beneficial agreement.

5. Be professional: While negotiating, be professional and avoid becoming defensive or aggressive. Remember that this is a conversation, not a confrontation, and that the goal is to find a mutually beneficial agreement.

6. Avoid discussing salary too early: If possible, avoid discussing salary too early in the interview process. Wait until you have a better understanding of the role and the company culture before bringing up salary.

D. Responding To Discriminatory Or Inappropriate Questions

Responding to discriminatory or inappropriate questions during a job interview can be uncomfortable and challenging, but it's important to handle the situation professionally and assertively. Discriminatory or inappropriate questions can be anything that relates to your personal information, such as your age, gender, race, religion, disability, sexual orientation, and more. Here are some tips for responding to such questions during a job interview:

1. Stay calm and composed: Take a deep breath and remain calm and composed. Don't let your emotions take over and avoid reacting with anger or frustration.

2. Redirect the conversation: Try to redirect the conversation back to the job requirements and your qualifications. Politely but firmly let the interviewer know that the question is not relevant to your qualifications for the position.

3. Be assertive: If the question is discriminatory or

inappropriate, be assertive in your response. You have the right to stand up for yourself and assert your boundaries.

4. Use humor or deflection: If appropriate, you can use humor or deflection to address the question without directly answering it. For example, you can say "I'm not sure how that relates to the job requirements, can we get back to discussing my qualifications?"

5. Be honest: If the question is not discriminatory but makes you uncomfortable, you can be honest with the interviewer and let them know that the question makes you uncomfortable. Be polite and professional when communicating your discomfort.

6. Know your rights: It's important to know your rights as a job applicant and employee. If you believe that you have been discriminated against during the interview process, you may want to seek legal advice or contact a human resources representative.

VIII. THE ART OF FOLLOWING UP

Following up after an interview is an important step that can set you apart from other candidates. Sending a thank-you email or note within 24 hours of the interview is a professional and courteous gesture that can leave a positive impression on the interviewer.

A. Sending Thank-You Notes

Sending thank-you notes after a job interview is a simple but effective way to leave a positive impression on the interviewer and demonstrate your professionalism and appreciation for the opportunity. A thank-you note can help to reinforce your interest in the position, remind the interviewer of your qualifications, and highlight any key points that you may have missed during the interview.

Here are some tips for sending thank-you notes after a job interview:

1. Send the note promptly: Send the thank-you note within 24-48 hours of the interview to ensure that it is received while the interviewer is still making their decision.

2. Address it to the right person: Address the thank-

you note to the interviewer or hiring manager who conducted the interview.

3. Personalize the note: Personalize the note and mention specific points from the interview. This can show that you were paying attention during the interview and are genuinely interested in the position.

4. Keep it concise: Keep the note concise and to the point. Thank the interviewer for their time, reiterate your interest in the position, and mention any key points that you may have missed during the interview.

5. Proofread: Proofread the note carefully before sending it to avoid any spelling or grammatical errors.

6. Use the right format: The format can vary, but you can choose to send an email or a handwritten note. An email is more convenient and faster, while a handwritten note adds a personal touch.

B. Inquiring About The Next Steps

Inquiring about the next steps after a job interview is an important part of the process and can help you to understand the timeline for the hiring decision and what to expect moving forward. By asking about the next steps, you can demonstrate your interest in the position and your proactive attitude.

Here are some tips for inquiring about the next steps after a job interview:

1. Ask at the end of the interview: If possible, ask about the next steps at the end of the interview. This can show your enthusiasm for the position and your eagerness to move forward in the process.

2. Ask about the timeline: Inquire about the timeline for

the hiring decision and when you can expect to hear back from the company. This can help you to manage your expectations and avoid unnecessary anxiety.

3. Ask about follow-up: Ask if there is anything you need to do to follow up or provide additional information. This can show your commitment to the position and your willingness to go the extra mile.

4. Be polite and professional: Be polite and professional when inquiring about the next steps. Avoid being pushy or demanding and show your appreciation for the interviewer's time and consideration.

5. Follow up if necessary: If you don't hear back from the company within the expected timeframe, follow up with a polite email or phone call. This can demonstrate your persistence and commitment to the position.

C. Handling Job Offers And Rejections

Handling job offers and rejections can be emotionally challenging, but it's important to approach both with professionalism and grace. Whether you receive a job offer or a rejection, it's important to respond in a timely and courteous manner.

Here are some tips for handling job offers and rejections:

1. Job Offers:
   - Review the offer: Review the job offer carefully and make sure that it aligns with your expectations and career goals.
   - Ask questions: If you have any questions or concerns about the offer, don't hesitate to ask for clarification. This can help you to make an informed decision.
   - Respond promptly: Respond to the job offer promptly

and with enthusiasm. Thank the employer for the opportunity and confirm your acceptance of the offer.

- Negotiate if necessary: If the offer is not quite what you were expecting, consider negotiating for a better salary, benefits, or other perks. Be polite and professional when negotiating.

2. Job Rejections:

- Don't take it personally: Rejections can be tough, but it's important not to take them personally. Remember that it's not a reflection of your worth as a person or a professional.

- Ask for feedback: If possible, ask for feedback on why you were not selected for the position. This can help you to improve your job search strategy and make better decisions in the future.

- Respond graciously: Respond to the rejection graciously and with appreciation for the opportunity. Thank the employer for considering you and express your interest in future opportunities with the company.

- Keep your options open: Don't get discouraged by a rejection. Keep your options open and continue to apply for other positions that align with your career goals.

IX. LEARNING FROM INTERVIEW EXPERIENCES

After an interview, it's important to reflect on your experience and identify areas where you can improve for future interviews. Here are some tips on how to learn from your interview experiences:

A. Analyzing Feedback

Analyzing feedback after a job interview is an important part of the job search process and can help you to improve your performance in future interviews. Feedback can come in many forms, such as written comments, verbal feedback, or evaluation forms. By analyzing feedback, you can gain valuable insights into your strengths and weaknesses and identify areas for improvement.

Here are some tips for analyzing feedback after a job interview:

1. Be open to feedback: Be open to feedback and don't take it personally. Remember that feedback is an opportunity for growth and improvement.

2. Look for patterns: Look for patterns in the feedback and

identify common themes. This can help you to identify areas for improvement that may be holding you back in the job search process.

3. Identify your strengths: Identify your strengths and focus on building on them. Feedback can help you to identify your unique selling points and communicate them more effectively in future interviews.

4. Set goals: Set goals for improvement based on the feedback you received. This can help you to stay focused and motivated in your job search.

5. Practice: Practice your interview skills and incorporate the feedback into your preparation. This can help you to build confidence and improve your performance in future interviews.

6. Thank the interviewer: Thank the interviewer for providing feedback and express your appreciation for the opportunity to improve.

B. Implementing Improvements For Future Interviews

Implementing improvements for future interviews is an important step in the job search process and can help you to improve your performance and increase your chances of landing the right job. By taking the feedback you received and identifying areas for improvement, you can develop a plan for enhancing your skills and communicating your unique selling points more effectively.

Here are some tips for implementing improvements for future interviews:

1. Focus on your weaknesses: Focus on the areas for

improvement identified in the feedback and develop a plan for enhancing your skills in those areas. This can involve practicing your interview skills, researching industry trends, or seeking mentorship or coaching.

2. Practice, practice, practice: Practice your interview skills with friends, family, or a career coach. This can help you to build confidence and improve your performance in future interviews.

3. Research the company and role: Research the company and role thoroughly before the interview to demonstrate your interest and knowledge of the company and position.

4. Prepare thoughtful questions: Prepare thoughtful questions to ask the interviewer that demonstrate your interest and understanding of the company and role.

5. Be authentic: Be authentic and genuine in your responses, and communicate your unique selling points and qualifications with confidence.

6. Follow up: Follow up with a thank-you note or email after the interview to demonstrate your professionalism and appreciation for the opportunity.

C. Building Your Professional Network

Building your professional network is an important part of the job search process and can help you to gain new insights, learn about job opportunities, and connect with industry professionals. By building your network, you can expand your reach and increase your chances of landing the right job.

Here are some tips for building your professional network:

1. Attend networking events: Attend networking events,

such as job fairs, industry conferences, or meetups. This can help you to meet new people and learn about industry trends and opportunities.

2. Join professional organizations: Join professional organizations related to your field or industry. This can help you to connect with like-minded professionals and gain new insights.

3. Use social media: Use social media, such as LinkedIn, to connect with industry professionals and learn about job opportunities. This can help you to expand your network and learn about new opportunities.

4. Volunteer: Volunteer for organizations or events related to your field. This can help you to gain new experiences, learn new skills, and meet new people.

5. Ask for introductions: Ask for introductions to people in your network who may be able to offer insights or job opportunities. This can help you to expand your reach and connect with new people.

6. Follow up: Follow up with people in your network and keep in touch. This can help you to maintain relationships and stay top of mind for future job opportunities.

X. CONCLUSION

J ob interviews can be nerve-wracking, but with the right preparation and mindset, you can stand out and secure your dream job. Throughout this book, we've covered various strategies and tips for acing the interview, from researching the company and role to mastering interview etiquette and showcasing your unique selling proposition. We've also discussed how to handle unexpected questions, address employment gaps and career changes, and discuss salary expectations.

It's important to remember that job interviews are an opportunity to showcase your skills and qualifications, but also to learn about the company culture and determine if the role is the right fit for you. By analyzing feedback, implementing improvements, and building your professional network, you can continue to grow and learn throughout your career.

Remember to approach job interviews with a positive mindset and to be authentic in your responses. You have valuable skills and experiences to offer, and by communicating them effectively, you can increase your chances of landing the right job.

Thank you for reading "Ace the Interview: Strategies to Stand Out and Secure Your Dream Job." We hope that the tips and strategies presented in this book will help you to feel more confident and prepared for your next job interview. Good luck in your job search! And before you go...

A. Emphasizing The Importance Of Continuous Learning

Continuous learning is an essential component of career growth and development. It allows individuals to stay up-to-date with industry trends, gain new skills and knowledge, and remain competitive in the job market. Emphasizing the importance of continuous learning is crucial for both job seekers and professionals.

Here are some reasons why continuous learning is important:

1. Stay current with industry trends: Continuous learning enables individuals to stay current with industry trends and changes, allowing them to adapt to new technologies and emerging fields.

2. Enhance career opportunities: Learning new skills and gaining new knowledge can open up new career opportunities and increase your chances of being considered for new positions.

3. Increase job satisfaction: Continuous learning can increase job satisfaction by providing individuals with new challenges and opportunities for growth and development.

4. Stay competitive: Continuous learning allows individuals to stay competitive in the job market by demonstrating their commitment to excellence and willingness to learn.

5. Personal growth: Continuous learning can promote

personal growth and development by expanding your knowledge and perspectives.

Here are some ways to promote continuous learning:

1. Attend workshops and seminars: Attend workshops and seminars related to your field or industry to gain new knowledge and insights.
2. Take courses: Take courses online or at a local college to enhance your skills and knowledge.
3. Read industry publications: Read industry publications and stay up-to-date with emerging trends and technologies.
4. Join professional organizations: Join professional organizations and attend events to network with like-minded individuals and gain new insights.
5. Seek mentorship: Seek mentorship or coaching from experienced professionals to gain new insights and perspectives.

B. Encouraging A Positive Mindset Towards Job Interviews

A positive mindset is essential for success in job interviews. When you approach an interview with a positive attitude, you're more likely to feel confident, perform well, and make a lasting impression on the interviewer. Encouraging a positive mindset towards job interviews can help individuals to overcome nerves, focus on their strengths, and communicate their unique selling points effectively.

Here are some tips for encouraging a positive mindset towards job interviews:

1. Visualize success: Visualize yourself performing well in the interview and landing the job. This can help you to build confidence and reduce nerves.

2. Focus on your strengths: Focus on your strengths and unique selling points, and communicate them with confidence.

3. Research the company and role: Research the company and role thoroughly before the interview to demonstrate your interest and knowledge of the company and position.

4. Practice, practice, practice: Practice your interview skills with friends, family, or a career coach. This can help you to build confidence and improve your performance in future interviews.

5. Stay positive: Maintain a positive attitude throughout the interview, even if you're feeling nervous or unsure. Smile, make eye contact, and be engaged in the conversation.

6. Learn from the experience: Regardless of the outcome of the interview, learn from the experience and use the feedback to improve your performance in future interviews.

www.ingramcontent.com/pod-product-compliance
Lightning Source LLC
Chambersburg PA
CBHW071111220526
45467CB00004B/1799